Bake through the Bible

Susie Bentley-Taylor & Bekah Moore

Design and illustration by André Parker
Edited by Alison Mitchell

Bake through the Bible
©Susie Bentley-Taylor and Bekah Moore/The Good Book Company, 2013. Reprinted 2014, 2018

Published by The Good Book Company
Tel (UK): 0333 123 0880, International: +44 (0) 208 942 0880 Email: admin@thegoodbook.co.uk
UK: www.thegoodbook.co.uk North America: www.thegoodbook.com
Australia: www.thegoodbook.com.au New Zealand: www.thegoodbook.co.nz

Cover photo and food photography by Susie J Stavert Food prepared by Tom Beard

Additional photography ©istockphoto.com ISBN: 9781909559004 Printed in India

Contents

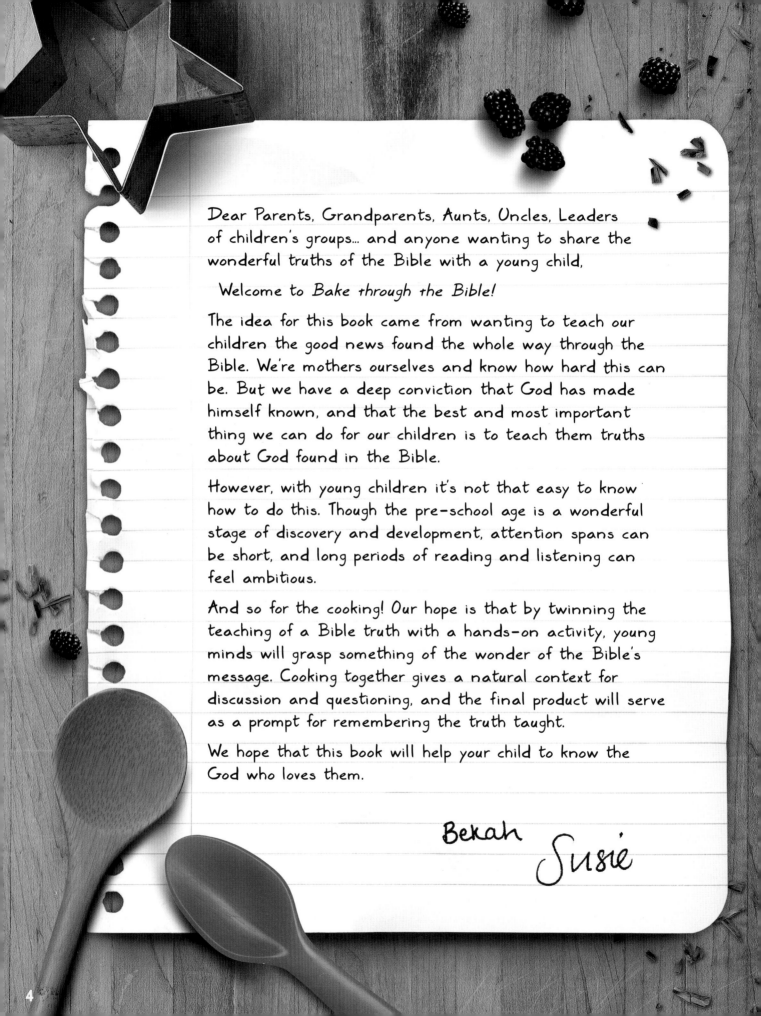

Dear Parents, Grandparents, Aunts, Uncles, Leaders of children's groups... and anyone wanting to share the wonderful truths of the Bible with a young child,

Welcome to *Bake through the Bible!*

The idea for this book came from wanting to teach our children the good news found the whole way through the Bible. We're mothers ourselves and know how hard this can be. But we have a deep conviction that God has made himself known, and that the best and most important thing we can do for our children is to teach them truths about God found in the Bible.

However, with young children it's not that easy to know how to do this. Though the pre-school age is a wonderful stage of discovery and development, attention spans can be short, and long periods of reading and listening can feel ambitious.

And so for the cooking! Our hope is that by twinning the teaching of a Bible truth with a hands-on activity, young minds will grasp something of the wonder of the Bible's message. Cooking together gives a natural context for discussion and questioning, and the final product will serve as a prompt for remembering the truth taught.

We hope that this book will help your child to know the God who loves them.

Bekah

Susie

How to use this book

Don't feel you have to be a good cook! Rather, we hope this is a way to include children in an activity that (to varying degrees) is a part of everyone's day-to-day life.

The cooking activities are designed to help unpack Bible truths for children. They are a means to an end. So it really doesn't matter if the cookies turn out a bit squishy or the pizza burnt round the edges. If a seed of biblical truth has been planted in a child's heart, praise God for that!

The book takes you through some of the Bible's storyline. It can be used as a starting point for a Bible overview, though each activity also works well on its own.

Each unit is made up of the following:

The Bible story

A story from God's word, simply explained, for you to read with your child.

Instructions

Look out for this symbol. ⚠ It shows steps that would be best done by an adult.

The cooking activity

This includes time-saving suggestions if you're pushed for time. See "Cooking with Children" on page 6 for more ideas.

While you cook

Questions to help your child understand the story. You may want to read the story and talk these through before beginning to cook—or you may choose to discuss them as you cook.

While you eat

A question to discuss once the cooking is done and the product finished. Your child might also like to use what they've cooked to tell someone else about the Bible story.

Cooking with children

Many children enjoy cooking from a very young age. It has numerous educational benefits: it encourages communication, develops motor skills and gives opportunity to practise listening skills and following instructions. Nevertheless, it can be a daunting prospect. Some parents feel they aren't very competent themselves in the kitchen, while others feel their children have too short a concentration span for any kind of cooking to take place successfully.

We want to assure you that cooking is possible for everyone! Some children will help their parents with a recipe from start to finish. Others will help mix the ingredients for a few seconds before getting distracted, and then return later to lick the bowl clean.

The level of participation doesn't really matter. If your child has enjoyed the experience, you can consider it worthwhile. And you might find you quite enjoy it yourself!

We want the cooking activities to help reinforce the wonderful truths of the Bible. So if you can find just one way to involve your child with the baking—and then use the finished product to talk about the Bible truth it goes with—what a success! If your hot cross buns are flat, your jelly boats crooked or your sad pizza faces burnt—and yet you've both had fun and you've been able to share how wonderful God is with your child—what a success!

We hope the following tips will encourage you to bake through the Bible with your child.

Prepare your recipe

Look at the recipe and any time-saving tips, and decide how much you'd like to do.

Decide which steps your child will help you with, and which you'll do before you call your child in to help you.

Work out when it will be best to do your recipe. Some recipes can be done in two parts, sometimes over two days.

Prepare your ingredients

You may want to involve your child in checking which ingredients you don't have and shopping for them. The shopping lists for each recipe are available to download—see page 60 for web details.

Decide whether your child can help you weigh out/cut the ingredients or if you should do it before they come in to help.

Prepare your kitchen

Move anything dangerous out of your child's reach. Also, look out for the "warning" symbol ⚠ used in some recipes to show steps that would be best done by an adult.

Find an apron or old clothes for your child.

Consider sitting at the table, maybe with your child fastened in a booster seat, to encourage them to sit still.

As well as the equipment listed for each recipe, consider buying a small rolling pin (large ones can be dangerous if dropped or thrown), reusable non-stick lining parchment (to save time greasing and lining tins), and a portable timer (so your cookies won't burn while you're upstairs putting the washing away).

Be prepared for lots of mess. That way, you won't be frustrated when that bowl of flour falls onto the floor!

Baking tips

Separating an egg (p8, 13, 40)

Carefully break an egg in half over a bowl. Then pass the yolk from one half of the egg shell to the other, so that the white falls into the bowl but the yolk stays in the shell.

Kneading dough (p15, 45)

Sprinkle the surface and your hands with a little flour. Shape the mixture into a ball; then punch it to lose any air. Put your hand into the dough and push it forwards, then pull it backwards. Turn it around and push and pull again for about 10 minutes. Your dough should become soft and springy.

God makes everything

(Genesis 1: Creation)

There was once a time when our world wasn't here. And then it was, because God made it. Wow! God just had to say, "Let there be light", and there was. It was good! That was the first day of creating things.

On the second day, he made the sky. That was good too. On the third day, he made the land, sea and plants. On the fourth day, he made the sun, moon and stars. On the fifth day, he made all kinds of colourful fishes and flapping birds. On the sixth day, he made tiny insects and amazing animals and wow! It was all good!

And then, God created in an extra special way. He made creatures who could get to know him and be his friends. And who were they? People, like you and me. God made the first man and the first woman. They were called Adam and Eve. When God looked at what he had made this time, he didn't just think it was good. He thought it was VERY good indeed.

On the seventh day, God rested and enjoyed everything he had made.

Pray: Lord God, help us to see and remember that you have made everything there is. Help us to be thankful to you for it. Thank you for making _____. Amen.

Creation cookies

It's amazing how many kinds of things there are in God's world! See how many different shapes you can make.

Ingredients (for 16 cookies)

- 300g/2 cups plain or all-purpose flour
- 150g/3/4 cup caster or superfine granulated sugar
- 250g/1 cup soft butter, cubed
- 1 large egg yolk (see page 7)
- 2 tsp vanilla essence
- ½ tsp salt
- Icing pens

Equipment

- Mixing bowl
- Wooden spoon
- Clingfilm/plastic food wrap
- Rolling pin
- Cookie or play-dough cutters
- Baking tray or cookie sheet, greased and lined with parchment
- Cooling rack

Time needed
60 mins

1.

Beat the butter and sugar together in the bowl.

2.

Then add the vanilla essence and egg yolk and beat until smooth. Add the flour and salt and mix it all together.

3.

Use your hands to shape the mixture into a ball. Wrap it in clingfilm/plastic food wrap and put it in the fridge for 30 minutes.

6.

Decorate your shapes using icing pens.

5.

⚠ Put the cookies in the oven for 12 minutes. Then put them on the cooling rack.

4.

⚠ Preheat the oven to 180°C/350°F/ gas 4. Sprinkle a clean surface with flour and roll the mixture until it is ½cm/¼" thick. Cut out different shapes and put them onto the baking tray.

While you cook...
- What are some of the things that God made?
- What must God be like to have made the whole world?
- Why are people extra special?
- Why is it good to say "thank you" to God?

Time-saver

Use ready-made cookie dough

While you eat...
Talk about all the amazing things that God has made.

God's people disobey him

(Genesis 3: The fall)

Take a look around you, or out of the window. What can you see? God made it all!

God had filled his world with all kinds of wonderful things. He had made tall trees and pretty flowers, roaring lions and wiggly worms. God had also made the first man and the first woman. They were called Adam and Eve. God made just one tree that Adam and Eve were not to eat from. It was called the tree of the knowledge of good and evil. If they did, they would die. It was God's way of reminding them that he's in charge and he knows best.

One sad day, a snake spoke to Eve. "Surely you don't really think you'll die if you eat the fruit from that tree!", it said. Eve knew that

God didn't ever lie, but it was so tempting to believe what the snake said. And so she did the one thing that God had told her not to do. She ate from the one tree she was not allowed to eat from. How sad. It was her way of saying: "I don't want God to make the rules. I want to make them myself." Adam ate from it too. Then they felt sad, guilty and ashamed.

God was not pleased with what Adam and Eve had done. He punished Adam and Eve and sent them away from his beautiful garden. He wanted them to know how terrible it is not to do what he says and not to be his friends.

Sad pizza faces

Disobeying God makes us feel sad, guilty and ashamed because God always knows best.

Pray: Lord God, help us to be sorry for the ways that we disobey you. Help us to remember that you always know best. Sorry for _____ . Amen.

Ingredients (for 4 pizzas)

- 2 English muffins, split in half
- 4 tbsp tomato sauce/pizza sauce
- 50g/¾ cup grated cheese
- A selection of toppings such as sliced olives, halved cherry tomatoes, pepperoni, sweetcorn, sliced peppers

Equipment

- Cheese grater
  (or use pre-grated cheese)
- Chopping board
- Sharp knife ⚠
- Baking tray or cookie sheet

Time needed
15 mins

1. ⚠ Collect your ingredients. Preheat the grill (broiler) to a medium heat or preheat the oven to 180°C/350°F/gas 4.

2. Spread the tomato sauce over the muffin halves.

3. Make your sad faces. Try tomato noses, cheese hair, olive eyes and pepper mouths.

4. ⚠ Put your pizzas on a baking tray/cookie sheet under the grill or in the oven until the cheese has melted.

Time-saver

Use ready-made cheese and tomato pizzas.

While you cook...

- What did God tell Adam and Eve not to do?
- What did they do?
- Why did Eve eat the fruit?
- How do we disobey God?
- What can we do about it?

Super-healthy tip

Make a yummy tomato sauce packed with vegetables. Cut 3 red peppers and 3 red onions into wedges. Roast them in a hot oven for 20-30 minutes until soft. Then whizz in a blender or food processor with a carton or jar of tomato passata. You can freeze any left-over sauce for up to a month.

While you eat...
Explain why your pizza has a sad face.

God makes amazing promises

(Genesis 12 & 15: Abraham)

Adam and Eve had disobeyed God. They had done just what God had told them not to do. Then things went from bad to worse. There were more people in God's special world. But they didn't love each other and they didn't love God. No one deserved to be treated kindly by God.

But God is VERY kind. So kind that he made some amazing promises. He gave them to a man called Abraham.

"I promise that there will always be people who trust in me. People beginning with your family," God said. "So many people that you won't be able to count them. Just like you can't count the stars in the sky!"

"I will show great kindness to these people. Through them I will show kindness to the whole world!" God said.

"And I promise that I will give these people a land to live in," God said.

And God is so great and so wonderful that he can keep all his promises. Even big ones like these!

Pray: Lord God, thank you for the wonderful promises you made to Abraham. Thank you that you are kind even when we don't deserve it. Amen.

Sparkly promise cookies

Try counting the sparkles on these cookies. Too many to count? Let that remind you of one of God's amazing promises!

Time-saver
Put promises under ready-made cookies and sprinkle with glitter.

Ingredients (for 12 cookies)

- 2 eggs
- 50g/¼ cup caster or superfine granulated sugar
- Pinch of salt
- 50g/¼ cup butter
- 50g/⅓ cup plain or all-purpose flour
- Few drops vanilla essence
- Small sprinkling of edible glitter

Equipment

- Mixing bowl
- Wooden spoon
- Small saucepan
- Baking tray or cookie sheet, greased and lined with parchment
- Palette knife/spatula
- Promise strips (see step 1)

Time needed 45 mins

1.

⚠ Preheat the oven to 180°C/350°F/gas 4. Write some of God's promises on 12 small strips of paper, or see page 61 for promises to copy.

2.

Separate the eggs (see page 7), keeping the white part. You don't need the yolks for this recipe. Stir the sugar into the egg whites and add the salt. Mix well.

3.

Melt the butter in a small saucepan or in the microwave and pour it into the eggs. Then add the flour and vanilla and beat it all together until smooth.

6.

⚠ Place a promise in the middle of each cookie and fold over using a palette knife/spatula. Hold for a few seconds until it keeps its shape. Carefully sprinkle each promise cookie with a little edible glitter.

5.

⚠ Put the cookies in the oven for 4 minutes, until the edges have turned brown.

4.

Drop the batter onto a greased baking tray/cookie sheet, using a spoon. The cookies need to be 5cm/2" apart. Spread the batter into a circle with the spoon.

While you eat...
Explain why the sparkles on your cookies remind us of God's promises to Abraham.

While you cook...
- How did people treat each other and God?
- What was one of the promises God made to Abraham?
- Does God always keep his promises?
- Why can we trust God?

God's people grow

(Genesis 18 & 21: Isaac)

God had made some big promises. He had promised that there would always be people who would trust in him. And he had promised that these people would start with Abraham and his children. But there was a problem. Abraham didn't have any children! And he was a very old man. Older than the oldest person you can think of. His wife was very old too. He didn't think he would ever have any children. He was old enough to be a grandpa. Even a great-grandpa! Surely he was too old to be a dad.

Abraham waited and waited. He waited for a very long time. Then one day, God said:

"Next year, you will have a son". His wife Sarah laughed. But God said: "Nothing is too hard for me!"

God was right. A baby boy was born, just as God said. Abraham was one hundred years old! They called the baby Isaac. Isaac grew up and had children. Then they grew up and had children. Then they grew up and had children, and so it went on. The number of God's people was growing, just as he had promised!

Pray: Lord God, thank you that you always keep your promises. Help me to learn to trust you more and more. Help me to trust you when I feel _____ . Amen.

Bread shapes

When you see that the dough has grown, let it remind you that God keeps his promises!

Ingredients (for 12 shapes)

- 500g/4 cups white bread flour
- 7g sachet/0.25 package fast-action dried yeast
- Pinch of salt
- 2 tbsp/30ml of olive oil
- 150ml/2/3 cup cold water
- 150ml/2/3 cup boiling water
- Extra flour and oil for sprinkling

Equipment

- Large bowl
- Wooden spoon
- Baking tray or cookie sheet, greased
- Clean, damp tea towel or oiled cling film/plastic food wrap

Time needed
30 mins
(plus 1 1/2hrs rising, growing time)

1. Mix the flour, salt, olive oil and yeast together in the bowl with a wooden spoon. Then stir in the water.

2. Mix everything together with your hands until it becomes a ball.

3. Sprinkle some flour onto a clean surface and tip the dough out onto it. Knead the dough with your hands for 10 minutes (see page 7).

4.  Wipe some oil around the inside of the mixing bowl. Place the dough in the bowl. Cover the bowl with the tea towel or clingfilm/plastic wrap and put it in a warm place.

Time-saver

Use a packet of bread mix and follow the instructions

5.  Leave the dough for about an hour: it should double in size. Wow! Then place the dough on the floured surface again and knead it for a minute so that it shrinks again.

Shape ideas

You can shape the dough into anything you like. Why not try sticks, round rolls, plaits or braids, swirls or a figure of eight?

6.

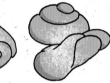

Shape the dough into different shapes. Place the shapes onto the tray, with plenty of space between them for the dough to grow again.

7.

Cover the shapes with the tea towel or clingfilm/plastic wrap and leave for 30 minutes for the dough to grow again.

8.

⚠️ Preheat the oven to 200°C/400°F/gas 6. Put the bread shapes in the oven for 15 minutes, until golden.

While you cook...

- Who did God make big promises to?
- Why was it hard for Abraham to trust God?
- When do you find it hard to trust God?
- Why can we always trust God?

While you eat...
Talk about how God kept his promise
to Abraham that his people would
grow in number.

God rescues his people

(Exodus 7-15: The exodus)

The number of God's people grew and grew and grew. But they were stuck in a country where they were made to work like slaves. They hated it.

God had a rescue plan. He spoke to a man named Moses. "Tell the ruler of this country to let my people go free," he said. And the ruler said… "NO. No way." So God turned the water in the river to blood to show that he is most powerful. Then he sent Moses to ask the ruler again. And still he said… NO. Then God sent frogs, but he still said NO. Then gnats. NO. Flies. NO. Disease. NO. Boils. NO. Hail. NO. Locusts. NO. Darkness. NO. Last of all, God said that the eldest child in every family would die unless the ruler changed his mind.

Lamb burgers

The very special meal that God's people ate in Egypt was called the Passover. The lamb was served with flat bread, because they were in a hurry and didn't have time to wait for it to rise.

At the same time, God gave some special instructions to his people. This was so that they could be sure that they would be kept safe.

"Kill a lamb," God told them, "and put its blood on your front door. Then I will keep your family safe. Cook and eat the meat and some bread as quickly as you can. Hurry! Tonight you are going to escape!" Yes, the lamb would die instead of the eldest child.

Everything happened exactly as God said it would. God helped his people to escape. He even made a path through the sea for them. Imagine seeing the crashing, splashing sea like that! What an amazing rescue. What a lot there was to thank God for. And that's just what Moses did.

Pray: Lord God, thank you that you rescued your people. Thank you that you sent Jesus to be our Rescuer. Help us to remember all that you have done for us. Amen.

Ingredients (for 8 burgers)

- 3 slices white bread
- 400g/14oz lamb mince (if lamb mince/ ground lamb is difficult to find, ground beef could be used as a substitute, but explain to your child that the meat eaten at Passover was lamb)
- Zest and juice from 1 lemon
- 1 tsp dried mint
- 1 tsp mustard
- 1 tbsp/15ml oil

Equipment

- Food processor
- Frying pan
- Mixing bowl
- Wooden spoon
- Clingfilm/plastic food wrap

- Unleavened bread such as pitta bread, to serve
- Salad, to serve

Time needed
50 mins

1.

⚠️ Whizz the bread to fine breadcrumbs.

2.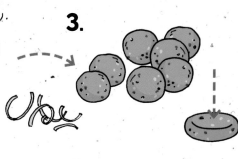

Mix all the ingredients, except the oil, together with the wooden spoon.

3.

Divide the mixture into eight using your hands. Shape the mixture into balls, then carefully flatten each to make a burger.

6.

Serve the burgers with the pitta bread and salad.

5.

⚠️ Heat the oil in the frying pan over a medium heat. Fry the burgers for four minutes on each side or until cooked through.

4.

Put the burgers onto a plate and cover with clingfilm/plastic food wrap. Put the burgers in the fridge for 30 minutes to firm up.

While you cook...

- How did God's people feel about being slaves?
- What were some of the things God sent to show how powerful he is?
- Why did God tell his people to put the blood of a lamb on their front doors?
- Who did God send to be our rescuer?

Time-saver
Use ready-made lamb burgers

While you eat...
Explain how God used the lamb to protect his people.

God shows us how to live
(Exodus 20: The 10 commandments)

Can you follow instructions? Try these ones: Clap your hands five times. Wiggle your fingers. Touch your toes. God had some instructions for his people that were far more important than these ones.

God had rescued his people from the land of Egypt. He spoke to Moses on the top of a mountain. "I am the One who rescued you," he said. "You've seen how big and powerful I am. Now I am going to give you some instructions to follow." God knew the best way for his people to live. He gave them these ten commandments:

- Do not let anyone or anything become more important to you than me.
- Do not try and make pictures or models of me and worship them.
- Do not use my name wrongly.
- Keep one day in the week a special day of rest.
- Love and obey your parents.
- Do not kill anyone.
- Do not take somebody else's husband or wife to be your own.
- Do not steal.
- Do not tell lies that make other people look bad.
- Do not be jealous of things that other people have.

The people were amazed that God had told them how best to live and to enjoy knowing him.

Pray: Lord God, thank you that you show us the best way to live. Sorry for the times when we get it wrong, like _____. Thank you that Jesus can help us to obey you. Amen.

Frozen fruit treats

God shows us the best way to live. These frozen treats need us to do a lot of waiting. We might get fed up with waiting, but following the instructions is the best way!

Ingredients (for 4 treats)

- 6 tbsp/90 ml blueberry, cranberry or red grape juice
- 6 tbsp/90 ml orange juice
- 3 kiwi fruits
- 3 tbsp/45ml cold water

Equipment

Time needed
15 mins
(plus 4 ½hrs freezing time)

- Measuring jug
- Four ice lolly/popsicle moulds
- Four lolly/popsicle sticks (Do not use the lids for the moulds with this recipe) Make sure the sticks will be able to stand upright in your freezer—you may need to cut them down a little.
- Blender or masher
- Sieve

1.

Pour out the grape/cranberry/blueberry juice to partly fill the moulds. Put the moulds into the freezer for 1 ½ hours.

2.

Pour out the orange juice between the moulds, on top of the first juice. Put the moulds into the freezer for 1 hour.

3.

Take them out and put a lolly stick into each mould. Put the moulds back into the freezer for 30 minutes more to set fully.

6.

Remove the lollies/popsicles from the moulds. If they won't pull out easily, hold the moulds under cold running water for a few seconds until they become loose.

5.

Pour the kiwi fruit liquid into the moulds to fill them. Put them in the freezer for 1 ½ hours until fully set.

4.

Blend or mash the kiwi fruit. Then push the fruit through a sieve to remove the seeds. Add the water and mix well.

While you cook...

- Where did God speak to Moses?
- How does God say people should treat him in instruction number one?
- How does God say people should treat each other?
- Why is it good to follow God's rules?

While you eat...

What would have happened if you hadn't left the lollies/popsicles in the freezer for all those hours? Why is it best to follow God's instructions?

Time-saver
....
Just make two layers instead of three.

God gives his people a home

(Joshua 5 & 6: Joshua)

God had promised to give his people a land of their very own. Now it was time for this to happen.

He chose a man called Joshua to be their new leader. Joshua led them to a big river. God made a path through the water and the people crossed into the new land. Splish splash! They came to a big city called Jericho. God had promised they could live there. But other people were already inside. So God gave Joshua some special instructions.

"For the next six days, tell your army to march once around the city walls. On the seventh day, march around the city seven times. Tell the priests to blow their trumpets and all my people to shout. Then the walls of the city will come tumbling down."

Joshua followed all of God's instructions. For six days, the army marched. Left, right, left, right. Then came the seventh day. The army marched around the walls not once, not twice, but one, two, three, four, five, six, seven times.

The priests blew loudly on their trumpets. Toot toot! The people shouted at the top of their voices. Then, just as God had said, there was the most enormous… CRASH!

And with more crashing and banging and clattering and tumbling, the walls of Jericho came falling down. God's people ran into the city. It was theirs! Then God helped them to take over more and more of the land that was their new home.

Pray: Lord God, thank you that you always keep your promises. Thank you that you promise a home in heaven to everyone who trusts in you. Amen.

Bread homes

How amazing that God gives his people a perfect home!

Ingredients (for 2 portions)

- 2 slices of brown bread
- 2 eggs

Equipment

- Baking tray or cookie sheet, greased and lined with parchment
- Small boy or girl cookie cutter
- Small plate

Time needed
15 mins

1.

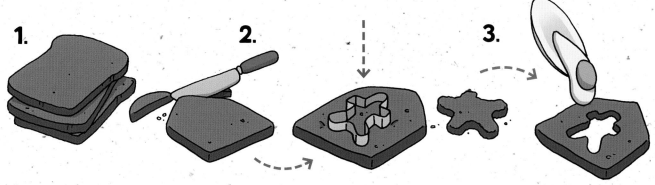

⚠ Preheat the oven to 180°C/350°F/gas 4. Cut off the top corners of each slice of bread to make it look like a house.

2.

Press the cutter into the middle of each house to make a person-shaped hole. Put the houses onto the baking tray/cookie sheet.

3.

Carefully break an egg onto a small plate. Tip the egg into the person-shaped hole. Repeat with the other egg.

4.

⚠ Put the bread and eggs into the oven for 8 minutes or until the yolk is set. Leave to cool slightly before eating.

While you cook...

- Who did God choose to be the new leader of his people?
- What instructions did God give to Joshua?
- What happened to the walls of Jericho?
- What did God give to his people?
- Where does God promise that his friends can live in the future?

While you eat...
Use your egg person in its bread home to tell the story of God giving his people a new home.

God looks after his people

(Psalm 23: A song of praise)

God's people had lived in their new land for many years. Then they asked God for a king. God gave his people a king called David. His job was to lead them and help them to love God, the real and best King of everyone. David wrote lots of songs about how great God is, including this one:

God, you are like a shepherd who perfectly looks after your sheep.

You give me everything I need.

You lead me to fields of delicious grass and pools of refreshing water.

You give me peace in my heart.

You show me the best paths to travel on and the best ways to live.

Even when life seems really difficult, I don't need to be scared, because you are always with me and you will look after me.

You are so kind to me and give me so much more than I deserve.

Surely goodness and love will be with me until I die. Then I get to be with you, God, in heaven. For ever!

Do you like singing? Why not try making up a tune for this song? Or sing it to a tune you already know!

Pray: Lord God, thank you for all the ways you look after us, like _____ . Thank you especially for the gift of your Son, Jesus, so that we can be friends with you and live with you for ever. Help us to look forward to that! Amen.

Thirst-quenching smoothies

How kind of God to look after us every day! And how wonderful that he knows exactly what we need!

Ingredients (for 4 glasses)

Peach and Strawberry Smoothie:
- 2 bananas, peeled and roughly chopped
- 2 peaches, peeled, stoned and roughly chopped (or a small can of peaches, drained)
- 8 strawberries, hulled
- 10 ice cubes

Mango and Banana Smoothie:
- 1 medium mango (or a small can of mangoes, drained)
- 1 banana
- 400 ml/1 3/4 cups orange juice
- 4 ice cubes

Equipment

- Blender or liquidiser
- Sharp knife

Time needed
5 mins

1.

Prepare all the ingredients for your smoothie.

2.

⚠ Put all the ingredients into the blender and whizz until smooth.

3.

Keep your smoothie in the fridge and drink on the day you make it.

While you cook...

- How is God like a perfect shepherd?
- Why don't we ever need to feel scared?
- How does God look after us day by day?
- How will he look after us when we die?

Time-saver
Use a ready-made smoothie and add ice cubes.

While you eat...
As you drink your refreshing smoothie, why not make a list of all the ways that God looks after you?

God promises a Forever-King

(2 Samuel 7: God's promise to David)

Do you remember King David? He wrote lots of songs about how great God is. God's people enjoyed having David as their king.

David lived in a beautiful palace. "God should have a palace too," thought David. Then God spoke to David.

"Do you think I need you to build me a palace?" asked God. "I am the God who gives my people everything they need. You don't need to do something for me. Instead, I am going to do something great for you. It is far greater than anything you can do or build."

Wow! How great? Greater than really, really great!

God told David what his great promise was: "Your name will be remembered for ever. This is because I will make someone from your family King of my people. But he won't be any ordinary king. He will stay my chosen King for ever and ever!"

Wow! For how long? For ever and ever and ever!

David was amazed that God had such wonderful plans for his family and his people. Someone from his family would be God's Forever-King!

"You are so great, God!" he said. "There is no-one like you, and there is no God but you. How wonderful to know that everything you promise comes true!"

David knew God always keeps his promises. So God's Forever-King really would come!

Crown cookies

God made a promise to King David of a far greater future King: a Forever-King!

Pray: Lord God, thank you for your promise of a Forever-King. Thank you that you always keep your promises. Thank you that we can know your Forever-King: King Jesus! Amen.

Ingredients (for 16 cookies)

- 300g/2 cups plain or all-purpose flour
- 150g/¾ cup caster or superfine granulated sugar
- 250g/1 cup soft butter, cubed
- 1 large egg yolk (see page 7)
- 2 tsp vanilla essence
- ½ tsp salt
- Icing pens
- Small colourful fruit, such as blueberries or dried cranberries, for decoration
- Edible glitter

Equipment

- Mixing bowl
- Wooden spoon
- Clingfilm/plastic food wrap
- Rolling pin
- Cookie cutters
- Baking tray or cookie sheet, greased and lined with parchment
- Cooling rack
- A crown template on thick cardboard (see template on page 61)

Time needed
60 mins

1.

Beat the butter and sugar together in the bowl.

2.

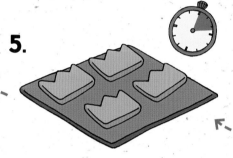

Then add the vanilla essence and egg yolk and beat until smooth. Add the flour and salt and mix it all together.

3.

Use your hands to shape the mixture into a ball. Wrap it in clingfilm/plastic food wrap and put it in the fridge for 30 minutes.

6.

Decorate your crowns using the icing pens to make outlines. Stick on the fruit using the pens. Sprinkle the glitter over the cookies to make them sparkly.

5.

⚠️ Put the cookies in the oven for 12 minutes. Then put them on the cooling rack.

4.

⚠️ Preheat the oven to 180°C/350°F /gas 4. Sprinkle a clean surface with flour and roll the mixture until it is ½cm/¼" thick. Then use a knife to cut out crown shapes.*

Time-saver
··················
Use ready-made cookie dough.

While you cook...

- What did David want to do for God?
- Did God need David to do this?
- Whose family would God's Forever-King come from?
- How long does God say his special King will be King for?
- Does God keep all his promises?

While you eat...
Crowns are sparkly because kings are important. Talk about God's promise of the most important King.

*You can use the template from page 61 as a guide).

God promises a Rescuer

(Isaiah 53)

God's people didn't just need a King. They needed a Rescuer. You see, God had told them how to love him and each other but they didn't do that. They didn't even want to do that.

God cared too much to just say: "Oh, never mind". They deserved to be punished. But God is so kind. He promised to send a Rescuer to put things right. Who could it be? It was… God's Forever-King! HE would be the Rescuer too. And this is what God said about him:

People won't love him because of what he looks like on the outside.

In fact, they will hate him and won't treat him like a king at all.

But this won't stop him loving us.

He will die,

Not because he has ever done anything to deserve it.

We deserve to die because of the things that we have done to hurt God and others.

But he will die to take the punishment that was meant for us.

And so we can have the friendship with God that only he deserves.

This is all God's idea—and it doesn't stop there.

God's Rescuer won't stay dead.

He will come back to life again!

And then he will rule as God's King and our Rescuer for ever and ever.

God's promised Forever-King would also be God's promised Rescuer!

Pray: Lord God, sorry for the ways we hurt you and hurt other people. Thank you that you sent your Rescuer, Jesus, to take the punishment we deserve. Help us to love him more and more. Amen.

Happy crêpe faces

God's people didn't do what God said and so deserved to be punished. Because God is so loving and kind, he promised to send them a Rescuer. Now that's something to be happy about!

Ingredients (for 4 crêpes)

- 100g/⅞ cups plain or all-purpose flour
- pinch of salt
- 1 egg
- 225ml/8 fl oz milk
- 1 tbsp vegetable oil
- 4 tbsp yogurt
- 4 tbsp bran or crushed Shredded Wheat
- Canned or dried apricots
- 8 large raisins or sultanas
- 2 bananas, peeled and sliced lengthways

Equipment

- Mixing bowl
- Hand mixer
- Frying pan
- Ladle

Time needed
15 mins

1.

Mix together the flour, salt, egg and milk in the bowl with the mixer until smooth

2.

⚠ Heat the oil in the frying pan over a medium heat until sizzling. Add a ladle of mixture and tip the pan until the bottom is covered.

3.

Leave the crêpe to cook for 2 minutes, then turn over and cook the other side for 1 minute. Put the crêpes on a plate; then repeat until the mixture is used up.

6.

For the nose, use an apricot round side up, and use a banana half for the mouth.

5.

For the eyes, put 2 apricot halves, round side down, below the hair. Then put a raisin inside each eye.

4.

To make the hair, spread one spoon of yogurt at the top of each crêpe. Then sprinkle the bran or shredded wheat onto the yogurt.

Time-saver
Use ready-made crêpes or pancakes.

While you cook...

- What did God's people need?
- Who deserves to be punished by God?
- What did God promise that his Rescuer would do?
- Who is God's chosen Rescuer?
- What can we say to God for being so kind and loving?

While you eat...

Why can we be very happy about God's promise of a Rescuer?

The birth of Jesus

(Luke 1 & 2)

How do you feel when you have to wait for something for a long time? Perhaps for the end of a long journey, or for your birthday. God's people had been waiting for something for a long time. A VERY long time...

God had promised a special King. Someone who would be King for ever and ever. Years and years went by. God's people waited and waited and waited. But God knew just the right moment. And now... it had come.

God sent an angel to give an important message to an ordinary woman. Her name was Mary.

"God is so kind!" the angel said. "He will give you a special job in his amazing plans! You don't need to be frightened. You are going to have a VERY special baby. You must call him Jesus (which means, "God rescues"). He will be the most special baby ever to have been born.

He is God's chosen Forever-King. He is God's own Son!" WOW.

"I want to serve God", Mary replied. She felt so happy and excited that she sang a song. "How great God is!" she sang. "La la la!"

Mary travelled with her husband, Joseph, to a tiny little town called Bethlehem. They looked for somewhere to stay. Knock knock! No room there. They tried again. Knock knock! No room there either. So they had to stay in a stable. A barn meant for animals, not people!

And in that not very special place, the very special baby was born. God's most precious gift. The gift of his one and only Son. Jesus.

Pray: Lord God, thank you that you are SO kind that you gave such a special, precious gift. You gave your Son, Jesus. Help us to love him more than any other present we might be given. Amen.

Christmas cupcakes

God's promised Forever-King and Rescuer has arrived. Let's celebrate the birth of Jesus!

Ingredients (for 12 cupcakes)

- 300g/2 cups plain or all-purpose flour
- 2 tsp baking powder
- 1½ tsp mixed spice or pumpkin pie spice (optional)
- 150g/¾ cup caster or superfine granulated sugar
- 50g/⅕ cup butter, cubed
- 225ml/8 fl oz milk
- 1 egg
- 2 tbsp/30ml jam or fruit jelly
- Selection of coloured ready-rolled icing or pre-made cake frosting
- Small dried fruit, icing pens, small sweets or edible shoe-laces to make a "J" shape

Equipment

- Mixing bowl
- Wooden spoon
- Sieve
- Small saucepan
- Cooling rack
- 6 cm/2½" circle cookie cutter
- Standard 12-hole muffin pan or tin with cases

Time needed
60 mins

1.

⚠ Preheat the oven to 200°C/400°F/ gas 6. Sieve the flour, baking powder and mixed spice into the mixing bowl. Then stir in the caster/superfine sugar.

2.

⚠ Put the butter and half of the milk into a pan. Put it onto a low heat until the butter melts. Then add the rest of the milk.

3.

Break the egg into the mixing bowl, add the milk and butter and stir until it is all just combined. Then spoon the mixture into the muffin cases.

Time-saver

Use ready-made cupcakes and add the icing (step 5).

4.

⚠ Put the cupcakes in the oven for 15 minutes. Then put them on a wire rack to cool.

If using icing...

5.

Put the jam or fruit jelly in the microwave for 20 seconds until it melts. Then spread the cooled cupcakes with a thin layer.

6.

Roll out the icing (using icing/powdered sugar so it doesn't stick to the work surface). Then cut out 12 circles, and stick these to the top of your cupcakes.

If using frosting...

7.

Make a "J" for Jesus on the top of each cupcake with your decorations.

Spread each cooled cupcake with a smooth layer of frosting.

While you cook...

- What had God's people been waiting for?
- Who did God send an angel to speak to?
- What did God say would happen to Mary?
- What can we say to God for giving us such a wonderful gift?

While you eat...
Talk about why the birth of
Jesus means we can be very
happy and celebrate.

The shepherds and the star

(Luke 2 & Matthew 2)

Baby Jesus had been born. Hooray! God had given the world the gift of his Son. He was God's special King and Rescuer. Who would hear about him first?

God sent an angel to share his wonderful news. Did he send the angel to tell the richest people? No. The really strong and powerful people? No. God sent his messenger to a group of very ordinary people: shepherds. The shepherds were REALLY frightened when they saw the messenger. They were used to seeing sheep, not angels!

"Don't be afraid," the angel said. "I'm here because I have fantastic news! News that's not just for you but for everyone. Today in Bethlehem, God's chosen Rescuer has been born. He is God's special King. He is God himself!"

Then, FLASH! Lots and lots more angels appeared in the sky. The whole sky lit up. They were full of happiness and sang about God's great news.

The shepherds went to see baby Jesus as quickly as they could. There he was, lying in a manger! They went home singing and talking and full of thanks to God. And they just couldn't help telling people about it. After all, it was the best news they had ever heard!

Starry jam tarts

The star led the wise men to God's Forever-King and Rescuer: Jesus!

Some time later, some wise men from a faraway country came to see Jesus. "We saw a bright star in the sky, and followed it to find the new King!" they said. It was a very, very long journey. But the star showed them exactly where to find Jesus.

They bowed down before him and gave him special presents. Gold: fit for a king. Frankincense: fit for someone who could go between God and his people. And myrrh: fit for someone who would one day die. Which is just what God had said would happen to his chosen Rescuer. But that wouldn't be the end of the story.

God's King, God's promised Rescuer, had arrived. Now that's worth celebrating!

Pray: Lord God, thank you that the news of your special King Jesus is for everyone. Help us to want to tell others about it, like the shepherds did! Amen.

Equipment

Time needed
30 mins

- Circle cookie cutter
- Star cookie cutter
- Standard 12-hole bun tin, greased
- Pastry brush

Ingredients (for 12 tarts)

- 1 tbsp flour
- 375g/16 oz pack ready-rolled shortcrust pastry/pie crust
- 12 tsp jam/fruit jelly
- 1 egg, beaten

1.

⚠ Preheat the oven to 200°C/400°F/gas 6. Sprinkle the flour onto a clean work surface. Unroll the pastry onto the flour.

2.

Cut out 12 circles and 12 stars. Push the circles into the muffin holes.

3.

Fill the circles with jam/fruit jelly and place a star on top of each.

5.

⚠ Put the jam tarts in the oven for 15 minutes and leave in the tin to cool.

4.

Brush the stars with the egg.

While you cook...

- Who did God send an angel to share his news with?
- What was God's great news?
- What did the shepherds do when they heard the news?
- What did the wise men do when they saw Jesus?
- Who can we share God's great news with?

While you eat...
Talk about how God first shared this great news that Jesus had arrived.

Super-healthy tip

Add fruit such as raisins, chopped apple, pear or strawberries to the jam/fruit jelly.

Jesus feeds thousands

(Mark 6 v 30-44)

Jesus the baby grew up to be Jesus the man. Just an ordinary man? Of course not! He was God's chosen King and Rescuer. He could do amazing things. Really amazing things.

One day, Jesus saw thousands and thousands of people coming to see him. He looked at them and felt so caring towards them. He knew that they needed someone to look after them. So he helped them by teaching them all kinds of things about God.

But there was another problem. They were getting hungry. "It's getting late!" said some of Jesus' friends. "Send these people away to find some food for themselves."

"You give them some food," Jesus said. Now how could they do that for all those people?

That's just what they thought. "Ha! We don't have enough money for that!" they said.

"Find out what food people have got with them," Jesus replied.

Was there enough for all the thousands of people? No way. Just one, two, three, four, five little loaves of bread and one... two little fishes. Hardly enough for one family!

Jesus told the people to sit down on the grass. Then he took the bread and the fishes and thanked God for them. He broke them into pieces and his friends started handing them out. Was there just enough for them? There was more than that. For the children? Still more. The people at the front? Still more.

And there just kept on being more and more and more and more until... Ahhh. All those thousands of tummies were stuffed full of food. There was even some left over! Wow. Jesus is amazing. He really can give us everything we need!

Pray: Lord God, thank you that Jesus is so amazing. Thank you that he looks after us by teaching us about you and giving us everything we need. Amen.

Spiral tuna wraps

Jesus is so caring and so amazing that he made one small picnic feed thousands of people!

Why not have a picnic with your friends to tell them what Jesus did and how amazing he is!

Here is one idea for your picnic. Then you can write a shopping list of other things you need to take with you.

Ingredients (for 5 wraps)

- 4 slices of bread, crusts removed
- 1 tsp butter or margarine
- 1 small tin of tuna
- 1 heaped tbsp mayonnaise
- Salad, to serve

Equipment

- Rolling pin
- Mixing bowl

Time needed
10 mins

1. Overlap two slices of bread by 1cm/½". Roll together with the rolling pin. Then spread the bread with butter.

2. Mix the tuna and mayonnaise together in the bowl, and then spread a thin layer over the butter.

3. Roll up the sandwich so that it looks like a long sausage. Then cut it into five sandwiches. Repeat steps 1-3 with the rest of the ingredients.

Super-healthy tip

Grate one or more salad vegetables, such as cucumber, and mix it into the tuna mayonnaise.

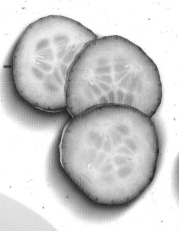

Time-saver

Use ready-made tuna sandwiches and cut them into fun shapes.

While you cook...

- Who did lots of people come to see?
- What was the problem?
- How much food could Jesus' friends find?
- What did Jesus do?
- So what is Jesus like?
- Why is it great to listen to Jesus?

While you eat...

Tell your friends how Jesus fed thousands of people with only one small picnic.

Jesus calms the storm

(Luke 8 v 22-25)

Can you make a sound like a roaring wind? How about heavy rain? And can you pretend to be someone being tipped from side to side in a boat? Use your sounds and actions as the story is told!

Jesus did all kinds of amazing things. After all, he was God's chosen King and Rescuer. God himself, in a man's body! One day, Jesus and some of his friends got into a boat. They wanted to get to the other side of a big lake.

SUDDENLY, the sky went grey. The wind started to blow. The boat started to rock. The rain started to pour and... help! Their little boat was caught in the middle of a terrible storm. The wind howled. The waves crashed and bashed and smashed against the side of the boat. The boat tipped from side to side, side to side. Whoosh! Crash! Whoa!! Then the waves got so big that... SPLASH! They came right into the boat. Jesus' friends were really, really frightened. And what was Jesus doing in all this? He was fast asleep!

Jesus' friends woke him up. "Save us!" they shouted. "We're all going to drown!" And still the wind roared and the waves kept coming.

"Why are you so afraid?" Jesus asked. Then he got up and looked out at the stormy waters. "Quiet! Be still!" he said to them. And the wind and the waves listened to him. Straight away, the storm stopped. The lake became as smooth as glass. "Why can't you trust me?" Jesus asked.

His friends were frightened and amazed. "Who is this man?" they said. "He can give orders to the wind and the waves, and they do what he says!"

Only God can do that.

Pray: Lord God, thank you that Jesus shows us what you are like. Help us to see how big and powerful you are. Help us to trust you more and more. Amen.

Jelly boats

Jesus told the wind and the waves to be still. And the roaring wind and big waves stopped still. Only God could do that!

(This recipe is quick to prepare but you will need to allow at least 6 hours setting time for the jelly/jello).

Ingredients (for 8 boats)

- 2 oranges, halved
- 1 pack of jelly/jello, your choice of colour
- 8 cocktail sticks
- 8 small paper triangles

Time needed
20 mins
(plus 6hrs setting time)

Equipment

- Orange squeezer/juicer (if you have one)
- Measuring jug
- Sharp knife ⚠

1.

Carefully squeeze the juice from each orange half, then set aside the juice to drink later.

2.

Use a spoon to scrape out as much flesh as you can. Place each orange half, open side up, onto a plate.

3.

Make up the jelly/jello according to the instructions on the packet.

6.

⚠ Cut the orange halves into half again, once the jelly/jello is completely set, to make eight boats. Push the sails into the boats.

5.

Write a "J" for Jesus on each triangle and carefully push a cocktail stick through the paper to make the sails.

4.

Pour it into the orange halves and put the plate into the fridge. Leave it to set for 6 hours.

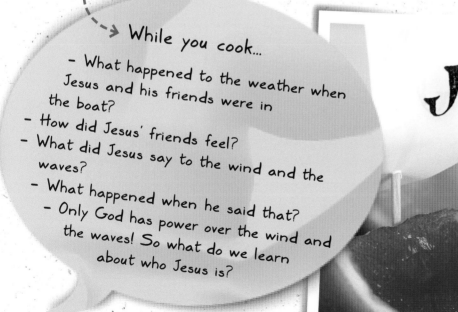

While you cook...
- What happened to the weather when Jesus and his friends were in the boat?
- How did Jesus' friends feel?
- What did Jesus say to the wind and the waves?
- What happened when he said that?
- Only God has power over the wind and the waves! So what do we learn about who Jesus is?

While you eat...
Use your boats to explain what Jesus did and why he could do it.

J

Jesus can open blind eyes

(Luke 18 v 35-43)

Close your eyes for a moment and imagine what it would be like not to be able to see anything.

A blind man was sitting at the side of the road. He couldn't see anything at all. He was begging. It was the only way he could get money. Would anybody walk by who might drop a few coins into his hands?

The blind man used his ears a lot, because his eyes didn't work. And his ears heard the sound of a crowd coming towards him. The chatter chatter of talking voices. The shuffle shuffle of walking feet. The crunch crunch of stones on the ground. And all getting closer and louder, closer and louder.

"What's happening?" he called out. He could hear a lot of noise but he couldn't see anything. He really wanted to know what was going on.

"Jesus is walking past," someone called back. Jesus!

"Jesus!" the blind man shouted. "You're the chosen Forever-King God promised to David! Be kind to me, Jesus!"

"Oh be quiet," said some of the people in the crowd. But that just made the blind man shout even louder. "JESUS! Be kind to me, Jesus!"

And Jesus listened. He stopped walking. He told some of the crowd to help the blind man to come right up to him. Then Jesus spoke to the man. "What would you like me to do for you?" Jesus asked.

"Lord, I want to see," said the blind man.

"Then see!" Jesus said. "You trusted in me, and so now I will make your eyes work!" And Jesus' words were all that was needed. Straight away, the man could see again. He was SO happy. He followed Jesus and thanked God. The people who were watching thanked God too!

Pray: Lord God, thank you that Jesus' words are so powerful. Thank you that he made the blind man see. Thank you that he can help people like us understand who you are. Amen.

See-through eyes

Jesus' words are so powerful that he could make the blind man see. These faces have eyes that melt and become see-through. They remind us that Jesus made the blind man see!

Ingredients (for 10 cookies)

- 300g/2 cups plain or all-purpose flour
- 150g/¾ cup caster or superfine granulated sugar
- 250g/1 cup soft butter, cubed
- 1 large egg yolk (see page 7)
- 2 tsp vanilla essence
- ½ tsp salt
- 20 boiled sweets/hard candies, various colours (such as Barley Sugars, Jargonelle Pears or Sherbet Lemons)
- Red icing pen

1.

Beat the butter and sugar together in the bowl.

2.

Then add the vanilla essence and egg yolk and beat until smooth. Add the flour and salt and mix it all together.

Time-saver

Use ready-made cookie dough.

3.

Use your hands to shape the mixture into a ball. Wrap it in clingfilm/plastic food wrap and put it in the fridge for 30 minutes.

4.

 Preheat the oven to 180°C/350°F/gas 4. Sprinkle a clean surface with flour and roll the mixture until it is ½cm/¼" thick. Cut out 10 large circles and place them on the baking sheet.

5.

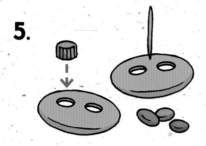

Cut out two eyes from each face using the bottle top. Place a boiled sweet/candy in each eye. Use the cocktail stick/toothpick to make a hole in the top centre of each face—not too near the edge or they will be too fragile to hang up.

6.

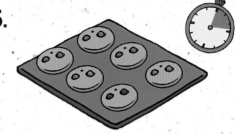

⚠ Put the cookies in the oven for 14 minutes. Then put them on a wire rack to cool. The sweets/candies should have melted to fill the hole and make the eyes see-through.

Smaller cookies

For smaller cookies, use small boiled sweets, such as sherbert pips. Use a circle for the eyes just a little bigger than the sweet (it needs space to melt), and a smaller cutter for the face.

7.

Draw a mouth on each face using the red icing pen. Thread a piece of string through each cookie so that you can hang it by a window. Now you can see through the eyes to remind you that God opened the blind man's eyes.

While you cook...

- Who did the blind man ask to help him?
- What did he understand about Jesus?
- How did Jesus make him better?
- What is Jesus like?

While you eat...

Can you remember what the blind
man believed about Jesus? And
what did Jesus do by just speaking
to the blind man?

Jesus dies

(Mark 15: The cross)

Jesus knew that he would have to die. He had said so to his friends again and again. Jesus was God's chosen Rescuer. He was the one God had promised a long, long time ago. And his death was God's amazing rescue plan! God's way of making it possible for people to be his friends.

Important Jewish leaders tried to find a reason to kill Jesus. They didn't believe that he was God's chosen Forever-King. They knew they had to get the powerful Roman rulers to agree with them if Jesus was going to die. So they got the crowds to join in. "Just kill him!" shouted the crowds. "Kill him! Kill him! KILL HIM!" The rulers were puzzled because they knew that Jesus hadn't done anything wrong. But they didn't want to upset the people. So they agreed.

They nailed Jesus to a wooden cross. Some people laughed at him. "If you're really God's special King, just set yourself free," they said. Jesus could have. But he didn't. He listened to God, not to people. He knew that this was all part of God's plan.

And so Jesus died on the cross. The sky went dark, even though it was the middle of the day. It was God's way of showing that he was punishing Jesus for all the ways people hurt God and each other.

Jesus' friends were very, very sad to see him die. But there was something they were forgetting. Something very important. Jesus had told them that he would see them again. And then they would be very, very happy!

Pray: Lord God, thank you for your great rescue plan. Thank you that Jesus died on the cross to take the punishment for the ways we hurt you and others, so that we can be your friends. Amen.

Hot cross buns

Jesus died so that we could be friends with God. The cross reminds us that Jesus has rescued us.

Ingredients (for 12 buns)

For the buns:
- 450g/4 cups white bread flour
- 1 ½ tsp fast-action dried yeast
- 200ml/7 fl oz milk, luke warm
- ½ tsp salt
- 1 tsp mixed spice or pumpkin pie spice
- 75 g/scant ½ cup caster or superfine granulated sugar
- 50g/4 tbsp butter, melted
- 1 medium egg
- 80g/¾ cup mixed fruit and peel
- Extra flour and oil for sprinkling

For the cross:
- 75g/¾ cup plain or all-purpose flour
- 4 tbsp/60ml cold water

For the glaze:
- 40g/scant ¼ cup caster or superfine granulated sugar
- 2 tbsp/30ml boiling water

Equipment

- Large bowl
- Wooden spoon
- Cookie or baking sheet,
  greased and sprinkled with flour
- Piping bag with nozzle
- Pastry brush
- Tea towel or clingfilm/plastic wrap

1.

Mix all the dry bun ingredients
together in a bowl and stir in
the melted butter.

2.

Mix the milk and egg in a jug
and gradually stir into the
other ingredients.

Time-saver

Get a pack of ready-
made hot cross buns
and use an icing pen
to ice over the lines of
the cross.

Hot cross buns shortcut

For 12 hot cross buns, mix one packet of white
bread mix with 1 tsp mixed spice/pumpkin pie spice,
75g/scant ½ cup caster or superfine granulated
sugar, 50g/4 tbsp melted butter, 1 egg and
80g/¾ cup mixed fruit and peel. Then follow the
instructions on the packet and jump in at step 7.

3.

Knead the dough on a floured
surface until it is soft.

4.

Wipe 1 tsp oil around the bowl and put the dough into it. Cover the bowl with a clean, damp tea towel/kitchen towel or some oiled clingfilm/plastic wrap and put it in a warm place.

5.

Leave the dough in a warm place to rise for 1 hour. Then shape the dough into 12 equal-sized buns. Place onto the cookie/baking sheet, with plenty of space between them for the dough to grow again.

6.

⚠ Cover the buns with the tea towel or clingfilm/plastic wrap and leave for 30 minutes for the dough to grow again. Preheat the oven to 200°C/390°F/gas 6.

8.

⚠ Dissolve the sugar in the boiling water to make a smooth glaze, and leave to cool slightly. Brush the glaze onto the buns.

7.

⚠ Mix the flour and cold water to form a smooth paste. Put the paste inside the piping bag, and pipe a cross onto each bun. Put the buns in the oven for 15 minutes or until golden. Then leave to cool slightly.

While you cook...

- What did Jesus know he would have to do?
- Who wanted Jesus to be killed?
- Whose plan was it that Jesus would die?
- What happened to the sky when Jesus died?

Time-saver

Instead of piping, use a sharp knife to cut a cross into each bun before baking.

While you eat...
Can you explain what the cross
reminds us about Jesus?

Jesus lives

(Luke 24 v 1-12: The resurrection)

Can you make a happy face? A sad face? How about a scared face? Why not use them to show how different people are feeling as the story is told?

Two days and two nights had passed since Jesus died on the cross. His body had been put into a tomb. The Roman rulers wanted to be very sure that no one could take the body. So they put a huge stone, taller than a man, in front of the entrance to block the way in. It was like a door that nobody could open. Some soldiers stood outside the tomb just to make extra sure that nothing happened. Well, that's what they thought…

Early the next day some women who were Jesus' friends went to the tomb. Wait a minute… Where was the huge stone? It had been rolled away! The women crept inside. But wait… Where was Jesus' body? They looked around again and again. It had gone! They were very confused.

SUDDENLY, two special messengers from God appeared beside them. They were wearing clothes that shone like lightning. The women were really scared. And the soldiers who were supposed to be strong and brave? They were

so frightened they were shaking! What was going on?

Then the messengers spoke to the women. "You're looking in a place meant for dead people for someone who's ALIVE!" they said. "Jesus isn't here. He isn't dead any more. He's alive again! Don't you remember? He told you that he would die and then live again!" They were right. Jesus HAD said this! WOW!

The women ran to tell more of Jesus' friends what they had seen. They felt so excited and still a bit scared, all at the same time. It all sounded so strange. Too good to be true!

A friend of Jesus called Peter wanted to see for himself. He ran to the tomb as fast as he could. His heart was racing and he was puffing and panting but he just had to find out… and sure enough, everything was just as the women had said.

Jesus wasn't lying in a tomb any longer. He was alive again. Really and truly alive! It was God's way of showing that YES! Jesus is his special, chosen Forever-King. Only he could come back to life after being dead. What a reason to celebrate!

Pray: Lord God, thank you that Jesus didn't stay dead, but that he is ALIVE! Thank you that now he is alive for ever and ever as your chosen Forever-King. Help us to celebrate this wonderful, amazing news! Amen.

Empty bread tomb with Easter dips

The tomb is empty: Jesus is alive! What a wonderful reason to celebrate. Let the bread tomb remind you that Jesus didn't stay dead. The dips are a special treat to celebrate this amazing news!

Equipment

Sharp knife ⚠️
Mixing bowl
Wooden spoon
Food processor or blender
2 small play figures (such as
Lego™ men)

Ingredients

For the bread tomb:
1 round "cob" loaf or another round
loaf of bread

Time needed
••••••••••
10 mins
(for bread tomb)

Turn the page for instructions on
making your tasty Easter dips...

1.

⚠️ Cut out a circular door in the side
of the loaf using the sharp knife.
Leave at least 4cm/2" between
the bottom of the door and the
base of the loaf.

2.

Cut off the bread behind the crust of the
door and set aside on a plate. Pull out
the bread from inside the tomb using your
clean hands and set aside on the plate to
use with the dips.

Empty tomb surprise

Why not make the bread tomb with your child the evening before? Place a toy figure inside,
for Jesus, and one outside, for a guard. In the morning, remove the figure from inside the
tomb before your child sees it, to remind them that Jesus is alive!

1. Guacamole

Ingredients
2 avocadoes, halved and stone removed; 1 small red onion, finely chopped (optional); 1 clove garlic, crushed; 1 ripe tomato, chopped; 1 lime, juiced.

Instructions
Scoop out the avocado from the skin using a spoon and mash it in a bowl using a fork. Add all the other ingredients and mix well. Season with salt and pepper.

2. Sour cream dip

Ingredients
200ml/1 cup sour cream; 100ml/½ cup mayonnaise; ½ tsp mustard; 2 drops Worcestershire sauce.

Instructions
Put all the ingredients into a bowl and mix well. Season with salt and pepper.

3. Tomato and basil houmous

Ingredients
1 can plum tomatoes; 1 can mixed beans; 1 small onion (optional); 1 clove garlic, crushed; ½ tsp salt; 1 tbsp basil; a pinch of cayenne pepper; 2 tsp olive oil.

Instructions
⚠ Whizz all the ingredients together in a food processor or blender until smooth.

Time-saver

Use ready-made dips.

While you cook...
- How did the Roman rulers try to make sure that nothing could happen to Jesus' body?
- What did the women find when they went to Jesus' tomb?
- Why was Jesus' body not there?
- Jesus really is alive! Why is that a reason to celebrate?

While you eat...
On Easter Sunday, we remember that Jesus didn't stay dead. Why is it such a happy day?

Jesus gives his friends a job

(Matthew 28 & Acts 1: The great commission)

Sometimes, people ask us to do things. It may be to put some toys away, or to get our shoes on. Jesus had a special job to give to his friends. He asked them to tell people about him.

Jesus had died on a cross but come back to life again. His tomb was definitely empty! And lots and lots of different people knew that this was true. They saw Jesus walk and eat and drink. They heard him talk and teach and pray. They knew that he was really and truly alive.

Jesus' friends were SO happy. Jesus had come back from the dead! That made him someone really special. They knew now that He was God's chosen Forever-King and Rescuer. They loved and praised him even more.

Jesus had important things to say to his friends. "God my Father has made me King over everything in heaven and on earth," he said. "Now it's your job to tell everyone everywhere about me."

The whole world needs to know that Jesus is the only One who can make people friends with God. That he is God's chosen Forever-King. And how can anyone know unless Jesus' friends tell them?

It was almost time for Jesus to go back to heaven. But that didn't mean he would leave his friends to get on with their job on their own. No way! God would send his Spirit to live inside them and be their special Helper. It would be just like having Jesus right there, but they wouldn't be able to see him.

"I'll always be with you," said Jesus. What an amazing promise! There wouldn't be one single minute of the day or night when Jesus wouldn't be right there with them. His friends needed to remember this as they got on with the job Jesus had given them.

Pray: Lord God, thank you that Jesus' friends have such wonderful news to share with everyone. Help us to be bold in telling others about him and help us to remember that you are ALWAYS with us! Please may _____ become one of your friends. Amen.

Fruity chocolate fudge gifts

What wonderful news we have to share with everyone! Let's make fudge to give to our friends who don't yet know Jesus. The fudge has a Bible verse on it that tells them how great Jesus is.

Ingredients (for 6 gifts)

- 300g/10oz milk chocolate, broken into pieces
- 200g/7oz plain/baking chocolate, broken into pieces
- 1 can of condensed milk (400g/14oz)
- 25g/1/8 cup butter
- 1 tsp vanilla essence
- 100g/4oz dried fruit, roughly chopped (colourful fruit such as cranberries or pineapple looks very pretty)

Equipment

- Non-stick saucepan
- Wooden spoon
- Square cake tin (about 15cm/6"), greased and lined
- Sharp knife or pizza wheel ⚠️
- 6 squares of greaseproof paper (20x20cm/8x8") or 6 cellophane confectionery bags
- 6 lengths of ribbon, 20cm/8"
- 6 pieces of paper about 6x6cm/ 2x2", with a hole punched in one corner

Time needed
45 mins
(plus 3hrs setting time)

1.

⚠️ Melt the chocolate, condensed milk, butter and vanilla essence in the pan over a gentle heat. Pour the fudge into the cake tin.

2.

3 hours

Arrange the dried fruit on the top, pushing it down slightly into the mixture. Put the tin into the fridge for three hours, or overnight, to set.

5.

Alternatively, put the fudge into cellophane confectionery bags. Tie with a length of ribbon, passing it through the hole of your tag.

4.

⚠️ Cut the fudge into 36 squares using the sharp knife or pizza wheel. Put 6 pieces of fudge in the middle of each square of greaseproof paper and gather the corners together.

3.

Ask an adult to help you write John 3 v 16 onto each tag. (Or use the templates on page 60).

While you cook...

- What job has Jesus given his friends to do?
- Who needs to know about Jesus?
- Who did God send to help Jesus' friends with this job?
- Who would you like to tell about Jesus?

While you eat...

Is there a special event at your church? Why not invite your friends to come? Then they can hear more about the wonderful news that Jesus is alive!

Jesus can make dirty hearts clean

(Acts 22: The change in Saul)

Think of the times when you get dirty. When your shoes need cleaning or your fingers get sticky. Perhaps it's when you've been outside in the mud and rain. Or inside with the paints and glue. Or in the kitchen doing some cooking!

Jesus said that everyone is dirty. Not the kind of dirty that you get when you've been playing with messy stuff. That sort of dirt can be washed off. No, Jesus said that people are dirty on the inside. We have dirty hearts. And how can we tell? Because we do and say things that are horrible and unkind. They make God sad. And no matter how hard we try, we just can't clean up our hearts. So how can they get clean? A man called Saul found out...

Saul's heart was very dirty. He was really horrible to anyone who said they were a friend of Jesus. He looked for ways to hurt them. He tried to get them put into prison. He HATED them because he hated Jesus. And then one day, he saw and heard something amazing.

A bright light burst from the sky. FLASH! It was so bright that Saul couldn't see anything. Then he heard a voice. "Saul!" the voice said. "Why do you hate me?"

Saul was so frightened that he fell to the ground. "Who's speaking?" he asked.

"I am Jesus," the voice said. Saul knew that he had to listen. Jesus was real and powerful! "Go to the city called Damascus," Jesus said, "and there you will be told what you need to do."

Saul did what Jesus said. In the city, he met a man called Ananias. "God is going to use you to tell many people about Jesus and how wonderful he is," said Ananias. "And now, what are you waiting for? Jesus is the One who can make your heart clean. You just have to ask him!"

That's just what Saul did. Jesus gave him a heart that wanted to love and listen to God. No amount of soap and water can do that!

Pray: Lord God, thank you that Jesus can make our hearts clean. Thank you that he can make us want to love and listen to you. Help us to do just that. Amen.

Dirty and clean hearts

How kind of God to show us that we have dirty hearts. And how amazing that Jesus can make them clean! These cookies have brown hearts and red hearts. Brown hearts are dirty. Red hearts are clean.

Ingredients (for 5 cookies)

- 300g/2 cups plain or all-purpose flour
- 150g/3/4 cup caster or superfine granulated sugar
- 250g/1 cup soft butter, cubed
- 1 large egg yolk (see page 7)
- 2 tsp vanilla essence
- 1/2 tsp salt
- 5 tbsp red fruit jam
- 100g/4oz dark or milk chocolate, melted, or 5 tbsp chocolate spread

Equipment

Time needed
60 mins

- Mixing bowl
- Wooden spoon
- Rolling pin
- Baking tray or cookie sheet, greased and lined with parchment
- Cooling rack
- Heart cookie cutter
- Circle cookie cutter, just bigger than the heart

1.

Beat the butter and sugar together in the bowl.

2.

Then add the vanilla essence and egg yolk and beat until smooth. Add the flour and salt and mix it all together.

3.

Use your hands to shape the mixture into a ball. Wrap it in clingfilm/plastic food wrap and put it in the fridge for 30 minutes.

4.

⚠ Preheat the oven to 180°C/350°F/gas 4. Sprinkle a clean surface with flour and roll the mixture until it is ½cm/¼" thick.

Time-saver
Use ready-made cookie dough.

5.

Cut out 15 circles. Cut out hearts from the middle of 10 circles.

6.

⚠️ Put the cookies in the oven for 12 minutes. Then put them on the cooling rack.

7.

While you cook...

- What does Jesus say our hearts are like?
- How can we know that we have dirty hearts?
- Who is the only One who can make our hearts clean?
- What needs to happen for our hearts to be made clean?

Spread the chocolate onto the 5 solid circles and stick 5 circles with heart-shaped holes onto them. Leave them for 15 minutes or until the chocolate is set, if using melted chocolate.

8.

Spread the jam onto the other side of the solid circles and stick the remaining 5 circles with heart-shaped holes onto them.

While you eat...

In fact before you eat... Put your biscuit on a plate with the "dirty" heart facing upwards. Can you explain what makes our hearts dirty? Now turn your biscuit over so that the "clean" heart is facing upwards. How can our hearts be made clean?

Clean hearts

Dirty hearts

God's new creation
(Revelation 19 & 21)

Think of all the things you love best about God's world. Sunshine or snow? People to talk to and play with? Delicious food? One day, God is going to make a new world. And it's going to be even better than all those things! It will be like this world and just as real, but PERFECT. A place that is happy and fun and exciting and special... because God will be there! And everything good that we enjoy is made by God.

So who will live there with God? God's friends. People who have asked Jesus to make their hearts clean. WOW. This is what God says his new world will be like...

At last! God and people will live together in perfect friendship. No one will do anything to hurt God or anyone else ever again. Everyone there will have hearts that God has made clean. And everyone there will love Jesus SO much. They will want to thank him and thank him and thank him for all his love and kindness. He died on the cross. He came back to life. He's the reason that God's friends can be there at all!

No one will cry ever again. Not even a single tear. There won't be anything that is sad or bad or scary or painful. No fighting, no arguing. No scratches, bumps or bruises. No feeling lonely or frightened or angry. No one will ever need to say sorry, because no one will ever make any mistakes. God's friends will just be loving and kind, because God will make them like that.

Being in God's new creation will be better than eating the most wonderful food in the world. It will be better than being in a beautiful, beautiful city made of pure gold and sparkling jewels. God's friends will understand just how amazing God is and love him as they should. Now that's DEFINITELY something to get excited about!

Pray: Lord God, thank you that you have promised that your friends can live with you for ever in the new world you will make. Help us to understand how amazing and exciting that is! Amen.

Banquet with gooey chocolate dessert

God's friends will live with him in his new creation FOR EVER! Make a banquet with your favourite foods to remind you that it's going to be AMAZING! Talk about what food you would like to have at your banquet. What is your favourite meal?

Here's an idea for dessert.

Ingredients (for 4 desserts)

- 4 dark chocolate muffins
- 4 chocolate bars (choose your favourite)
- For the filling, a selection of: sliced bananas, dried fruit, mini marshmallows, small cookie pieces

Equipment

- Sharp knife ⚠
- Small bowl

Time needed 10 mins

1. Cut a hole in the top of each muffin, using the sharp knife. Make the hole 3cm/1½" wide and half as deep as your muffin.

2. Melt the chocolate bars in the bowl in a microwave (or in a bowl over a pan of simmering water).

3. Fill the hole in the muffins with your choice of ingredients. Then pour the melted chocolate over your muffins.

While you cook...
- What has God promised he will make one day?
- Who will live with God in his new world?
- How will God's friends treat each other in God's new world?
- What can we say to God for promising something so amazing?

While you eat...
Can you tell the people at your banquet why living with God in his new creation is going to be SO amazing?

Downloads
Visit our website for downloads

1. Visit our website

2. Click on the download

3. Print and cut out your templates

thegoodbook.co.uk/baking thegoodbook.com/baking
thegoodbook.com.au/baking thegoodbook.co.nz/baking

Templates

Verse tags (p52)

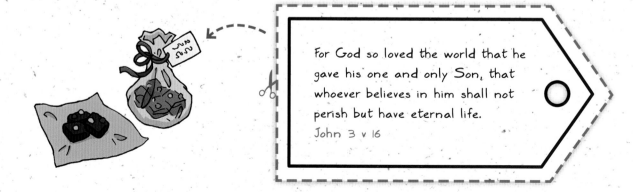

For God so loved the world that he gave his one and only Son, that whoever believes in him shall not perish but have eternal life.
John 3 v 16

Promises (p12)

God promised to Abraham:
There will be so many people who trust in me, you won't be able to count them! Genesis 15 v 5

God promised to his people:
I will never leave or abandon you. Deuteronomy 31 v 8

God promised to Abraham:
I will show great kindness to my people.
Genesis 12 v 2

Jesus promises to those who believe and trust in him:
I will give you rest when you bring your worries to me.
Matthew 11 v 28-29

God promised to Abraham:
I will show kindness to the whole world through my people. Genesis 12 v 2-3

Jesus promises to those who believe and trust in him:
You will not die but you will live with me for ever.
John 3 v 16

God promised to Abraham:
I will give my people a land to live in. Genesis 12 v 1

God promises to those who believe and trust in Jesus:
You will be saved from death. Romans 10 v 9

God promised to Abraham:
My people will be great. Genesis 12 v 2

God promises to those who believe and trust in Jesus:
Nothing can separate you from my love.
Romans 8 v 38-39

God promised to Abraham:
I will make you famous. Genesis 12 v 2

God promises to those who keep on believing and trusting in him:
I will be your God and you will be my children.
Revelation 21 v 7

Crown template (p26)

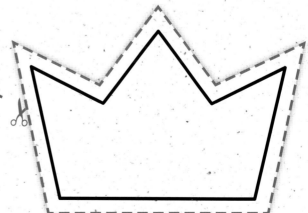

About the authors

Susie Bentley-Taylor now lives in London, having lived in Oxford for many years. She is married to Pete and they have two precious children: Joshua (4) and Molly (2). She loves Jesus, reading, writing, being outside and cooking (of course!)—both with and without the happy company of her children!

Bekah Moore grew up in South Yorkshire and, after spending many years in Oxford, she is now back north, in Hartlepool. She is married to Nick and they have two sons, Simeon (4) and Francis (2) who, like Bekah, love the beach, food and Jesus. They are part of the church family at All Saints Stranton.

Thank you

A huge thank you to the team at The Good Book Company for turning our idea into a reality, and for all their input along the way.

Thanks also to our husbands, Pete and Nick, for their support and encouragement, and to our children, Joshua and Molly, Simeon and Francis, for being enthusiastic participants throughout the whole process!

thegoodbook COMPANY

Bible-reading resources
for children and families

Bake through the Bible at Christmas

12 fun cooking activities to explore the Christmas story with young children.

Beginning with God

Bible-study notes for pre-schoolers with 44 colour stickers. Linked with *The Beginner's Bible* but can be used with any pre-schooler Bible.

XTB

Annual subscription available

Packed with puzzles, pictures, prayers and solid teaching for 7–10s. Twelve issues available.

Table Talk

Annual subscription available

Three months of Bible times to help families discover God's Word together.

www.thegoodbook.com/familybiblereading